HAPPY THOUGHTS & WISE WORDS
Positive Messages for Children
Hannah Rachael Hudd

Happy Thoughts & Wise Words
Positive Messages for Children
Copyright 2024 Hannah Rachael Hudd
ISBN 9798328663731

All Rights Reserved. No part of this publication may be reproduced, stored in a retrieval system, or transmitted, in any form or in any means – by electronic, mechanical, photocopying, recording or otherwise – without prior written permission.

Part One:

Pages 1 - 47: I am...

Part Two:

Pages 48 - 99

50: Emotions, Feelings, Moods,

60: What Makes ME Feel Good?

70. Friends, Family, & Relationships

78. Change

80. Time

82. Fear

88: Empathy – The Big Picture

96. I Am Creating My Future

PART ONE

Happy Thoughts & Wise Words

I am unique, special, and perfect!

There will never be another me!

Hannah Rachael Hudd

Happy Thoughts & Wise Words

I love and respect myself always!

I love and respect my family and friends.

I always try to treat everyone with respect.

Hannah Rachael Hudd

Happy Thoughts & Wise Words

I am capable and intelligent.

I am creative and talented.

My imagination is limitless!

I AM...
CAPABLE
INTELLIGENT
CREATIVE
TALENTED
IMAGINATIVE
LIMITLESS

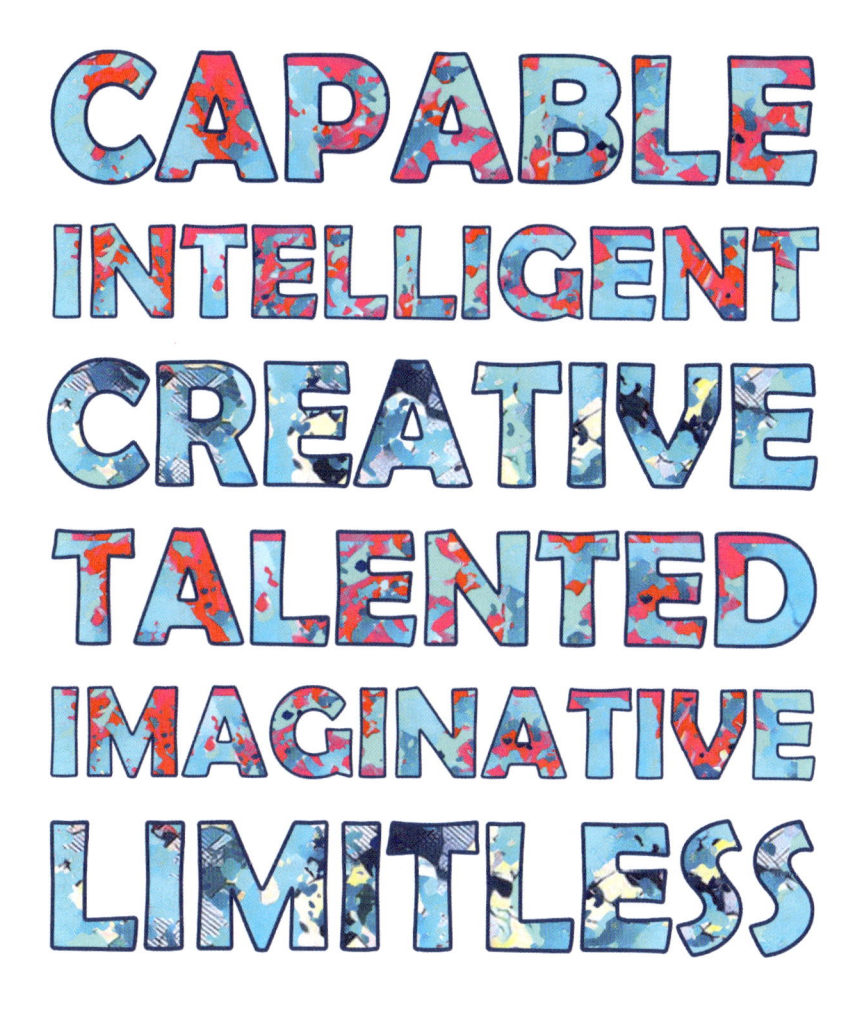

Hannah Rachael Hudd

I am gorgeous, inside and out! I am perfect just the way I am.

Beauty comes in all shapes, sizes, and colours! We are all beautiful in our very own special way.

We are all unique works of art!

I AM...

BEAUTIFUL
GORGEOUS
UNIQUE
SPECIAL
DIFFERENT

Hannah Rachael Hudd

Happy Thoughts & Wise Words

I am kind, fun, funny, thoughtful, and confident. Lots of people would love to be my friend.

To make true friends, I just need to be myself.

I am a wonderful person. I like myself a lot and I enjoy being me!

Hannah Rachael Hudd

I am helpful, kind, and generous.

I am honest and tell the truth.

Hannah Rachael Hudd

Happy Thoughts & Wise Words

I am safe and protected.

I am brave and confident.

I am strong and powerful.

I AM...
SAFE
PROTECTED
BRAVE
CONFIDENT
STRONG
POWERFUL

Hannah Rachael Hudd

My body is approximately 65% water! Like water, I can be as powerful as a crashing wave, or as calm and gentle as a lake.

I am learning to use my energy and power wisely!

Hannah Rachael Hudd

Happy Thoughts & Wise Words

My thoughts, ideas, and opinions are important.

I am important.

Everyone is important.

Everyone has different ideas and points of view.

I listen to other people and respect their opinion, even if I don't always agree.

Hannah Rachael Hudd

I try to be kind to everyone and encourage them to do their best!

The world would be a better place if everyone felt happy and confident.

Hannah Rachael Hudd

Happy Thoughts & Wise Words

I am lucky and fortunate.

It's important to realise how lucky we are and appreciate everything we have.

Sharing is caring! I share with my friends, family, and people who have less than me.

I AM...

LUCKY
FORTUNATE
APPRECIATIVE
CARING
GENEROUS

Hannah Rachael Hudd

Happy Thoughts & Wise Words

The hobbies and interests I love are perfect for me.

Sometimes I like doing things that other people like, sometimes I like being different.

Discovering our natural talents and finding out what we enjoy, makes us all cool, fun, and interesting!

Hannah Rachael Hudd

25

Happy Thoughts & Wise Words

My imagination is a wonderful world to explore.

My mind is a safe, happy place where I can think about things, solve problems, and entertain myself.

Hannah Rachael Hudd

27

I am full of ideas and thoughts that I can choose to share or enjoy just for myself.

Daydreaming is a fantastic way to imagine the world and the life I would like to create.

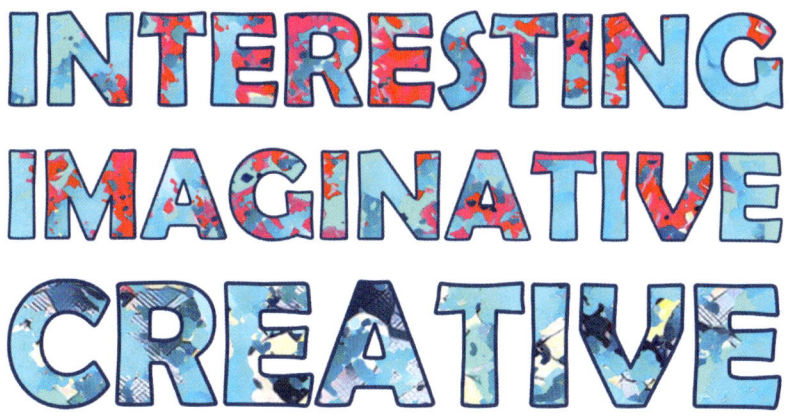

Hannah Rachael Hudd

Happy Thoughts & Wise Words

Every day is a new adventure.

The perfect opportunity to learn, play, and explore.

If I try my best, I can do anything!

Practice makes perfect!

Hannah Rachael Hudd

I love learning and I am a great student!

Learning is easy when I listen carefully, pay attention, and ask questions when I don't understand.

The more I learn, the easier it will be to make my dreams come true.

I AM...

INTELLIGENT
DETERMINED
CONFIDENT

Hannah Rachael Hudd

Everyone is talented and clever in their own way.

Everyone in my class is special in their own way.

We are all good at different things.

I AM...

TALENTED
CLEVER
SPECIAL
DIFFERENT

Hannah Rachael Hudd

Happy Thoughts & Wise Words

I am learning to look after myself with the help of my family, friends, and teachers.

I am learning to look after my friends, family, and pets.

I am learning to look after my things and to take care of our home, school, and community.

I AM...
RESPONSIBLE
CAREFUL
NEAT
TIDY

Hannah Rachael Hudd

I try to do my best for myself, my friends, and my family.

I do my best to look after animals, plants, and nature.

The planet Earth is our home, and we all need to take care of it.

I AM...

HELPFUL
KIND
CARING
RESPONSIBLE

Hannah Rachael Hudd

Happy Thoughts & Wise Words

I am learning to create happy friendships and relationships at home and at school.

I am creating a happy, healthy life by learning to make good decisions.

I AM...

HAPPY
FRIENDLY
HEALTHY
WISE

Hannah Rachael Hudd

Happy Thoughts & Wise Words

Everyone makes mistakes sometimes. The important thing is to learn from them and try to do better next time.

OOPS!

Sometimes, the most boring things are the most important things we need to do to help ourselves and others.

BORING!

Hannah Rachael Hudd

Happy Thoughts & Wise Words

I am lucky to have delicious food and drinks at home.

I try to choose healthy options to make me strong and give me lots of energy.

Every day I am stronger, fitter, happier, and healthier.

I AM...
LUCKY
HEALTHY
STRONG
FIT
HAPPY

Hannah Rachael Hudd

Happy Thoughts & Wise Words

I love playing and having fun but sometimes I need to rest to recharge my batteries!

I love sleeping so I can wake up with lots of energy for the day ahead.

When I fall asleep I have beautiful, happy dreams.

I AM...

CALM
RELAXED
HEALTHY
ENERGETIC

Hannah Rachael Hudd

Happy Thoughts & Wise Words

PART TWO

Happy Thoughts & Wise Words

EMOTIONS
FEELINGS
MOODS

Do you know the difference between emotions, feelings, and moods?

Hannah Rachael Hudd

Happy Thoughts & Wise Words

EMOTIONS

Emotions are a natural reaction that happens in your body.

When something happens, your brain releases a chemical that flows through your body and makes you feel happy, sad, excited, angry, scared...

Emotions happen quickly and don't normally last long.

They are automatic, physical reactions that we can't control.

Happy Thoughts & Wise Words

FEELINGS

Feelings are created when we think about our emotions, a situation, a relationship, or an event.

Feelings happen in our mind and in our body. We can learn to control our feelings because we can choose what we think about.

For example, if we feel sad or scared, or worried or angry, we can practice thinking about something positive and happy until we feel better.

We can ask someone we trust to help us or we can do something fun to cheer ourselves up!

Hannah Rachael Hudd

Happy Thoughts & Wise Words

MOODS

Our moods are how we feel in general. They can last a long time, sometimes they can last for days!

Our moods are affected by lots of different things.

For example...

- Our thoughts, emotions and feelings.

- Things that happen with our friends, family, teachers, classmates.

- Our health. What we eat and drink. How much we sleep and exercise.

Hannah Rachael Hudd

Happy Thoughts & Wise Words

- Our surroundings and even the weather!

The best way to improve our mood is to take care of our bodies and to practise thinking about positive, happy things.

Everyone is different, and we all respond to activities, events, and situations in our own way.

It is important for each of us to learn what makes us feel happy, relaxed, healthy, and safe.

Hannah Rachael Hudd

Happy Thoughts & Wise Words

WHAT MAKES ME

60

FEEL GOOD?

Hannah Rachael Hudd

Happy Thoughts & Wise Words

FEELINGS

Think about the following questions and what makes YOU feel good.

For each of the situations, think about...

What can you do? (or not do!)

Who can help you?

When I am tired, I feel better if I...

When I have too much energy and can't relax, I feel better if I...

Hannah Rachael Hudd

Happy Thoughts & Wise Words

FEELINGS

When I am...

sad
bored
lonely

I feel better if I...

When I am...

grumpy
confused
frustrated
angry

I feel better if I...

Hannah Rachael Hudd

Happy Thoughts & Wise Words

FEELINGS

When I feel...

scared
worried
embarrassed

I feel better if I...

When someone upsets me, I feel better if I...

If I upset someone, I feel better if I...

Hannah Rachael Hudd

Happy Thoughts & Wise Words

FEELINGS

If I am worried about something, or I have a problem, I can talk to someone I trust.

The people I trust most in the world are...

When I'm happy and full of energy, my favourite things to do are...

Hannah Rachael Hudd

Happy Thoughts & Wise Words

FRIENDS
FAMILY
RELATIONSHIPS

"To the world you may be one person; but to one person you may be the world."
— Dr. Seuss

Hannah Rachael Hudd

Happy Thoughts & Wise Words

FRIENDS

Some of us have lots of friends...

...and some of us only have one or two.

Sometimes, if we are having a bad day, we might feel like we don't have any at all!

But when it comes to friends, it's QUALITY, not QUANTITY, that counts!

The best way to attract good friends, is to practice BEING a good friend.

What do you think makes someone a good friend?

Hannah Rachael Hudd

Happy Thoughts & Wise Words

FAMILY

All families are different.

Some families are big and some are small. Some all live in the same place, while others live all over the world!

Some of us live with our families and some of us don't.

Sometimes families change over time.

Whatever our situation, we all have special people in our lives that care about us.

People who want us to be happy, healthy, safe, and comfortable.

Hannah Rachael Hudd

Happy Thoughts & Wise Words

FAMILY FRIENDS

Who are your favourite people (and pets!)?

Who takes care of you?

Who do you take care of?

Who can you speak to if you have a problem?

Who can you go to for help or good advice?

Who boosts your confidence and makes you feel good about yourself?

Who do you have lots of fun with?

Hannah Rachael Hudd

Happy Thoughts & Wise Words

CHANGE

Life can be full of surprises. Some are happy and some are sad, but whatever happens, everything is always OK in the end.

As we grow up, one of the most important lessons that we can learn is how to cope when things change.

Changes can be scary but they can also be exciting. They are opportunities to learn something new, meet new people, or try new things.

If you're worried, talk to an adult you trust for help.

Hannah Rachael Hudd

Happy Thoughts & Wise Words

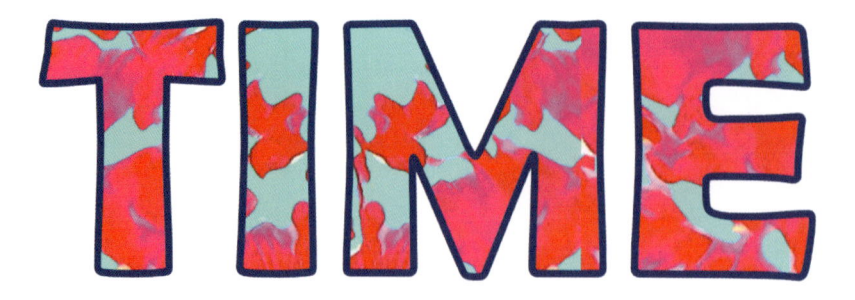

TIME

As well as our health, family, and friends, time is one of the most precious things we have!

Spending time with our favourite people is one of the best gifts we can give them.

What we choose to do with our time helps to create our future. So we should spend our time wisely!

Being young is fantastic!

We have lots of time to explore, experiment, and discover our talents.

Hannah Rachael Hudd

Happy Thoughts & Wise Words

FEAR

Feeling scared or nervous sometimes is natural. In fact, it can be a good thing!

Fear is our body's natural reaction to danger. When our brain thinks we might be in danger, it releases chemicals that flow through our body that make us feel scared or nervous.

These chemicals act like an alarm to warn us of potential risks or problems.

They wake up our senses so we are more aware of what is happening.

Hannah Rachael Hudd

Happy Thoughts & Wise Words

FEAR

Absolutely everyone feels scared or nervous sometimes.

We feel fear in our mind and our body.

When we feel scared or nervous, we need to pay attention to the messages that our brains are sending us.

They are trying to protect us so we need to listen carefully.

Sometimes it's a false alarm and there is nothing to worry about.

Hannah Rachael Hudd

Happy Thoughts & Wise Words

FEAR

But sometimes, our natural instincts are right and we need to be careful!

It is not brave or clever to ignore our natural alarm. In fact, in some situations it can be very dangerous!

So next time you feel scared or nervous, don't feel embarrassed, silly, or weak.

Just remember that your brain is keeping you safe by making you think before you act or take risks.

Fear helps us make better decisions and avoid danger.

Hannah Rachael Hudd

Happy Thoughts & Wise Words

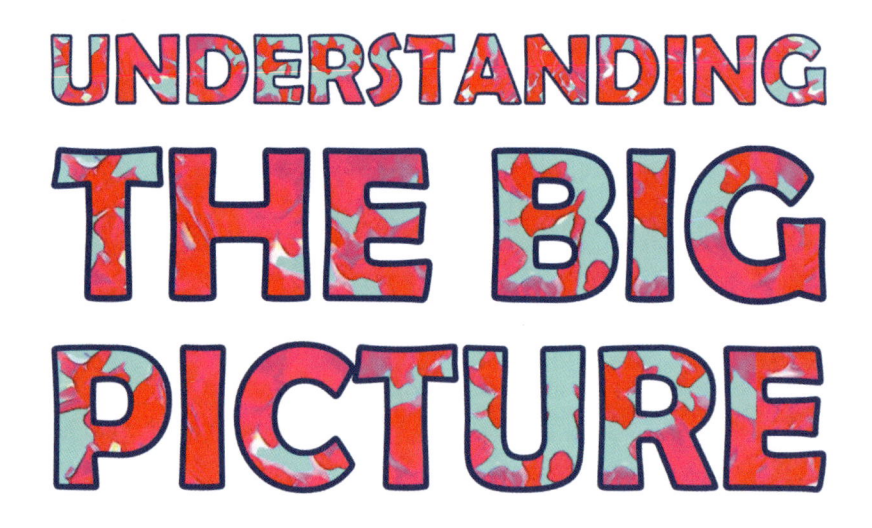

EMPATHY

UNDERSTANDING THE BIG PICTURE

Another important life lesson, is to learn to have empathy for other people.

When we are "empathetic" it means that we try to imagine how other people feel.

Hannah Rachael Hudd

Happy Thoughts & Wise Words

EMPATHY

When we try to understand others, it helps us have better relationships at home and at school.

It also helps us feel better about ourselves and not take everything personally.

For example, if someone is mean to us, our brains may release chemicals that flow through our body and make us feel sad or angry.

If we continue to think about these natural emotions, our sadness and anger might grow.

Hannah Rachael Hudd

Happy Thoughts & Wise Words

EMPATHY

Maybe we will start to feel other negative emotions too.

We might feel shy or embarrassed.

We might worry about other people's opinion of us.

Maybe we will start to feel jealous or think that everything is unfair.

If we continue to think about ourselves, it will affect our mood.

Once we are in a bad mood, we might be mean back or do something to upset someone else!

Hannah Rachael Hudd

Happy Thoughts & Wise Words

THE BIG PICTURE

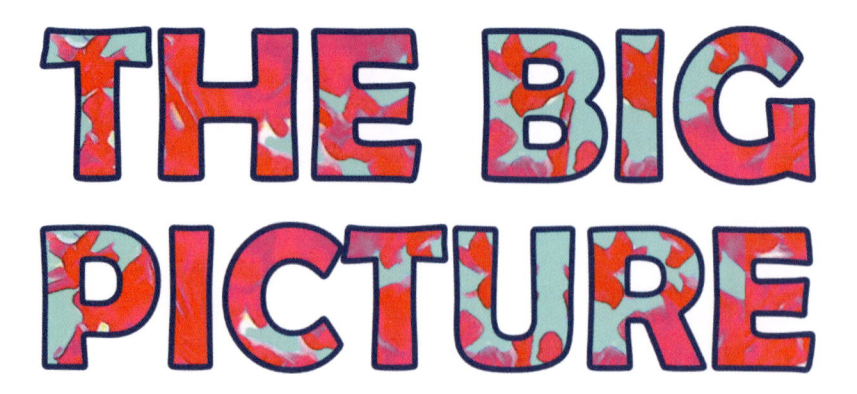

However, if we try to imagine how the other person feels, we might realise that they were only mean to us because they feel bad about themselves.

Maybe they are sad, jealous, angry, etc...

When we see the "big picture", we learn that not everything is about us. So we don't need to feel bad about ourselves.

Depending on the situation, we can try to help the person who was mean to us or leave them alone until they feel better.

Hannah Rachael Hudd

Happy Thoughts & Wise Words

I AM CREATING MY FUTURE

Although it might not always feel like it, we have a lot more control over our lives, than we think!

I AM...
POWERFUL
INTELLIGENT
WISE

Hannah Rachael Hudd

Happy Thoughts & Wise Words

I am learning to control my mind, body, and actions.

Everyday, I can choose what to do, say, and think.

Everyday, I can make good decisions that affect my health, happiness, friendships, and education.

I can grow up to be whoever I want to be.

If I follow my heart, work hard, and believe in my dreams, the sky is the limit!

Happy Thoughts & Wise Words

Visit the author's website for more resources & information.

100

Printed in Great Britain
by Amazon